Once Upon a Time

Writing Your Own
Fairy Tale

by Nancy Loewen

illustrated by
Christopher Lyles

PICTURE WINDOW BOOKS
Minneapolis, Minnesota

Editor: Jill Kalz
Designer: Nathan Gassman
Page Production: Melissa Kes
Editorial Director: Nick Healy
The illustrations in this book
were created with mixed media on illustration board.

Picture Window Books
151 Good Counsel Drive
P.O. Box 669
Mankato, MN 56002-0669
877-845-8392
www.picturewindowbooks.com

Printed in the United States of America.

All books published by Picture Window Books
are manufactured with paper containing
at least 10 percent post-consumer waste.

Library of Congress Cataloging-in-Publication Data
Loewen, Nancy, 1964–
Once upon a time : writing your own fairy tale /
by Nancy Loewen ; illustrated by Christopher Lyles.
p. cm. — (Writer's Toolbox)
Includes index.
ISBN 978-1-4048-5335-5 (library binding)
ISBN 978-1-4048-5336-2 (paperback)
1. Fairy tales—Authorship—Juvenile literature.
I. Lyles, Christopher, 1977- II. Title.
PN171.F35L64 2009
808'.066398—dc22   2008040536

Special thanks to our adviser, Terry Flaherty, Ph.D., Professor of English, Minnesota State University, Mankato, for his expertise.

A goose lays golden eggs. A frog turns into a prince. A magic beanstalk grows high into the clouds—where a giant lives!

What kinds of stories are these? Fairy tales, of course.

Fairy tales are very old stories with magical characters. Every culture has its own fairy tales. When the stories formed, few people could read or write. The tales were spoken out loud.

Let's take a close look at the story "Little Red Riding Hood." You'll see how the right tools can help you write your own fairy tale!

Once upon a time, in a woods far away, lived a little girl. She owned a red cloak with a hood. She wore it all the time. Everyone called her Little Red Riding Hood.

~ Tool 1 ~

The **SETTING** is the time and place of a story. In fairy tales, the setting is made up. The stories happen in the distant past. The place might be an imaginary forest, village, or castle. No real time or place is described. The setting of "Little Red Riding Hood" is a faraway forest, long ago.

4

~ Tool 2 ~

The **CHARACTERS** are the people or creatures in the story. The main character is the one who appears most often in the story. In this fairy tale, Little Red Riding Hood is the main character.

~ Tool 3 ~

The **PLOT** is what happens in a story. In fairy tales, the plot moves quickly. We don't learn much about Little Red Riding Hood. We don't learn much about her mother or grandmother. Instead, the action begins right away.

One day, Little Red Riding Hood's mother gave her a basket. "Here are some cakes and breads," her mother told her. "Take them to your grandmother. She is ill. The treats will give her strength."

As Little Red Riding Hood set off, her mother called after her. "Stay on the path!" she said. "Don't stop to play along the way!"

~ Tool 4 ~

DIALOGUE is what characters say to each other. Good dialogue helps move the story along. It gives the reader information.

~ Tool 5 ~

In fairy tales, characters often get **WARNINGS**, like the one given here by Little Red Riding Hood's mother. Warnings give the reader clues about what might happen later in the story.

"I'll be careful," the girl said.

Little Red Riding Hood walked deeper and deeper into the woods. After a while, she met a wolf. She didn't know that the wolf was a wicked creature, so she wasn't the least bit scared.

~ Tool 6 ~

All fairy tales contain **MAGIC.** That's one of the things that sets them apart from other old stories. Fairy tales can be about witches, giants, trolls, elves, and animals. They can be about kings and queens, princes and princesses. Objects, such as mirrors and clocks, can come to life. And, yes, fairy tales can be about fairies, too!

"Good morning,"
said the wolf.
"Where are you off
to on this fine day?"

"I'm bringing this basket of cakes and breads
to my grandmother," Little Red Riding Hood
explained. "She is ill, and these treats will
give her strength."

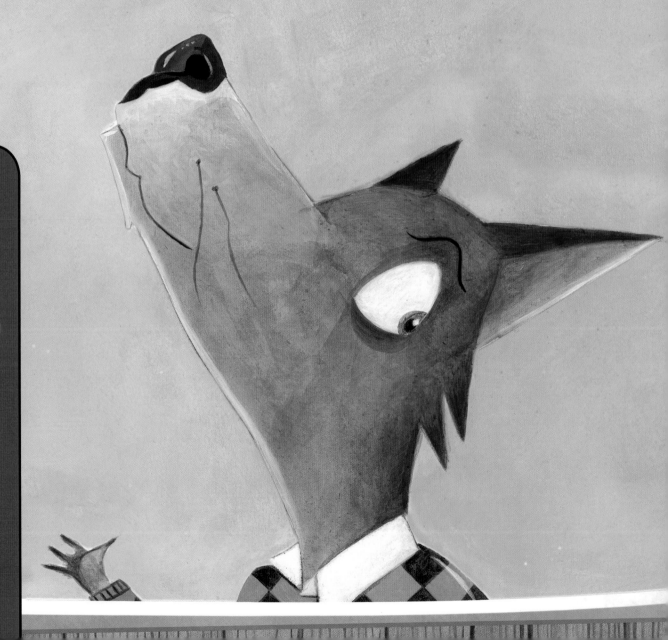

"Where does your grandmother live?" the wolf asked.

"She lives in a small wooden house farther up the path," Little Red Riding Hood said.

~ Tool 7 ~

Fairy tales often have characters who are filled with **GREED**. These characters want something that someone else has. And they will do anything to get it. Here the wolf wants an extra-big lunch. That means there's trouble ahead for Little Red Riding Hood!

The wicked wolf was very hungry. He wanted to eat both the girl and her grandmother for lunch. Quickly he thought of an evil plan.

~ Tool 8 ~

In fairy tales, characters often use **TRICKS** to fool each other. Little Red Riding Hood wants to do the right thing. But the wolf gets her thinking about the flowers. She ignores her mother's warnings and runs off to the field. The wolf's plan works perfectly.

"Your grandmother might like some flowers, too," the wolf suggested. He pointed to a clearing in the woods. "Look at that field. It has flowers of every color!"

"But Mother told me to stay on the path and not to stop," Little Red Riding Hood said.

"Nonsense!" the wolf said. "It will take just a minute. The flowers will cheer up your grandmother."

Little Red Riding Hood nodded. Her feet started edging off the path. "Yes," she said. "Yes, they will!" And she ran to gather flowers for her grandmother.

The evil wolf dashed off to the grandmother's house. He swallowed the poor woman whole! Then he put on her bonnet, got into her bed, and waited.

Before long, Little Red Riding Hood came skipping up the path. The front door was open, so she went right in.

"Hello! Grandmother!" she called. "I've brought you a basket of treats, and some flowers, too!"

~ Tool 9 ~

In many good fairy tales, the reader knows a **SECRET**—something the characters don't. Little Red Riding Hood has no idea that the wolf is in her grandmother's bed. But you do!

Little Red Riding Hood became uneasy when she looked at her grandmother.

"Grandmother," she said slowly. "What big ears you have."

"The better to hear you with, my child," the wolf said.

"Grandmother, what big eyes you have."

"The better to see you with, my sweet."

~ Tool 10 ~

The **REPETITION** of words or actions gives them more power. Using nearly the same words, Little Red Riding Hood notices the wolf's ears ... then eyes ... then teeth. The suspense builds. When the wolf jumps out of bed, the little girl is frightened, and so are we!

"And Grandmother, what big teeth you have!"

"The better to EAT you with!" the wolf snarled. He jumped out of bed and swallowed poor Little Red Riding Hood, too.

With his stomach filled, the wolf lay back down for a nap. He snored loudly.

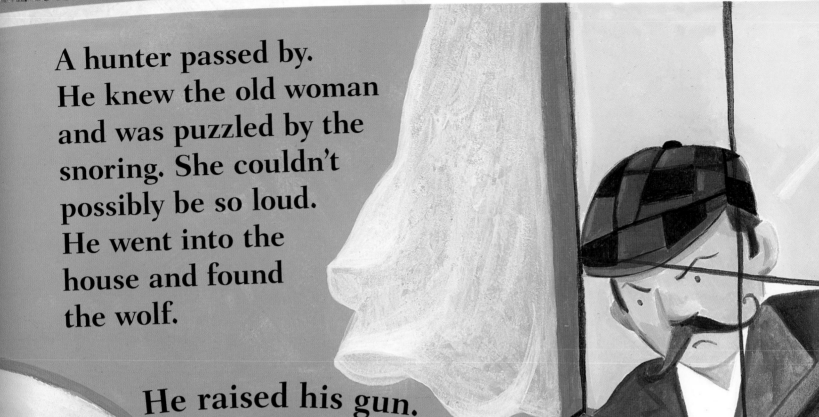

A hunter passed by.
He knew the old woman
and was puzzled by the
snoring. She couldn't
possibly be so loud.
He went into the
house and found
the wolf.

He raised his gun.

~ Tool 11 ~

In fairy tales, greedy
characters often make
MISTAKES. These
mistakes then lead to
their downfall. What if
the wolf hadn't taken
a nap?

Then the hunter noticed the wolf's big belly. He put down his gun, took out a pair of scissors, and cut open the wolf's stomach.

Out jumped Little Red Riding Hood. And out crawled the old grandmother.

~ Tool 12 ~

In some fairy tales, **PROBLEM-SOLVING** happens through luck or magic. That's what happens in this story. The hunter comes along at just the right time and stops the evil wolf. Little Red Riding Hood and her grandmother get out of trouble through luck.

In other fairy tales, characters get out of trouble on their own. They solve their problem by being brave, strong, or clever.

The three quickly filled the wolf's stomach with stones and sewed him back up. The wolf awoke and tried to run away. But he was too heavy to move!

He fell to the floor, dead.

The hunter went home with the dead wolf's skin.
The grandmother ate her treats and soon became well.

~ Tool 13 ~

Fairy tales come to a **PLEASING END.** They sometimes close with "And they lived happily ever after." The reader is left with the idea that nothing bad will happen to those characters ever again.

And Little Red Riding Hood promised that she would always listen to her mother and stay on the path!

THE END

Let's Review!

These are the **13 tools** you need to write great fairy tales.

Fairy tales take place in made-up times and places, or SETTINGS **(1)**. They usually begin, "Once upon a time" and have good and bad CHARACTERS **(2)**.

A fairy tale PLOT **(3)** moves quickly. Actions are more important than details. DIALOGUE **(4)** between characters often includes WARNINGS **(5)**.

Fairy tales include MAGIC **(6)**. A wolf blows down a house made of sticks. A gingerbread cookie comes to life. A fairy godmother turns mice into horses.

The bad characters in a fairy tale are often filled with GREED **(7)**. They use TRICKS **(8)** to get what they want.

The reader often knows a SECRET **(9)**, information the characters don't. The REPETITION **(10)** of words or actions can build suspense.

Bad characters usually make MISTAKES **(11)** that lead to their downfall. Good characters SOLVE THEIR PROBLEM **(12)** on their own, or through luck or magic, bringing the fairy tale to a PLEASING END **(13)**.

Getting Started Exercises

- ✏️ Look at the objects around you. Pick one. What if that object came to life? What would it do? What might it want? What special powers would it have?

- ✏️ Pick one or two words from each of the following sets. What does each word make you think of? Let those thoughts be the starting point of your story.
  - *queen, king, scarecrow, boy, girl, frog, butterfly, jellyfish, gorilla, cricket*
  - *marry, bake, chatter, dig, hop, hum, twist, gobble, poke, dance*
  - *lake, palace, seed, spoon, ticket, riddle, rope, quicksand, peach, freckles*
  - *skinny, smart, pink, fearful, lazy, windy, juicy, nervous, quick, brave*

- ✏️ Think of something you like, and play a "what if" game. Let's say your choice is ice cream. What if people ate ice cream all day long? What if someone stole all the ice cream in the world? What if ice cream gave people special powers? Play around with your ideas, and pretty soon you'll have a story!

Writing Tips

Fairy tales don't have a lot of details. But the details that are there are very important. Here's an example from "Little Red Riding Hood." After swallowing both Little Red Riding Hood and her grandmother, the wolf takes a nap. He snores loudly—so loudly that the hunter hears him! That one detail affects the whole story.

Have your characters talk to each other. Good dialogue gives life to your characters.

Fairy tales are about feelings that we all have. Think about what your characters are doing. Are they feeling love, courage, joy, anger, or fear? Your story will be stronger if your characters have strong feelings.

*

Glossary

character—a person or creature in a story

culture—a nation or group of people with shared beliefs and customs

detail—one of many facts about a certain thing

dialogue—the words spoken between two or more characters; in writing, dialogue is set off with quotation marks

greed—wanting more of something than is actually needed

magic—the power to control things with charms or spells

mistake—something done incorrectly

plot—what happens in a story

problem-solving—finding answers to things that cause trouble

repetition—doing, saying, or making something again and again

secret—information known only to oneself or a few people

setting—the time and place of a story

suspense—worry, unease

tricks—actions done to fool people

wicked—evil, bad, wrong

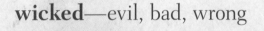

To Learn More

More Books to Read

Foreman, Michael. *Classic Fairy Tales.* New York: Sterling Pub., 2005.

Perrault, Charles. *Cinderella.* Mankato, Minn.: Creative Editions, 2000.

Zelinsky, Paul O. *Rapunzel.* New York: Dutton Children's Books, 1997.

On the Web

FactHound offers a safe, fun way to find educator-approved Internet sites related to this book.

Here's what you do:

1. Visit *www.facthound.com*
2. Choose your grade level.
3. Begin your search.

This book's ID number is 9781404853355

www.FactHound.com®

Index

Look for all of the books in the Writer's Toolbox series:

Once Upon a Time: Writing Your Own Fairy Tale
Show Me a Story: Writing Your Own Picture Book
Sincerely Yours: Writing Your Own Letter
Words, Wit, and Wonder: Writing Your Own Poem